MW00463157

Will the *Real* Jesus Please Stand Up?

Dennis Ingolfsland

™

Post Gutenberg

AN IMPRINT OF
GLOBALEDADVANCEPRESS

Will the Real Jesus Please Stand Up?

Copyright © 2014 by Dennis Ingolfsland

Ingolfsland, Dennis 1954 -

ISBN 978-1-935434-31-3

Subject Codes and Description:
Subject Codes and Description: 1. REL 006070 Religion – Biblical Commentary -- New Testament; 2. REL 006220 – RELIGION—Biblical Studies – New Testament;; 3. REL 067040 Religion: Christian Theology - Christology

NIV translation of the Bible was used in this book.
Cover design by Brian Lane Green
Printed in Australia, Brazil, France, Germany, Italy, Spain, UK, and USA.

Published by
Post-Gutenberg Books™
an imprint of
GlobalEdAdvance Press

www.GlobalEdAdvance.org

There was once a TV show called, "To Tell the Truth." It was a game show in which a panel of four celebrities was given the name and unusual occupation of one of three contestants. The panel had to ask the contestants questions in an attempt to determine which contestant performed the unusual occupation. At the end of the show the host would ask, "Will the real [contestant name] please stand up? Considering all the different views of Jesus presented in books, magazines and movies today, people today might feel like asking, "Will the real Jesus please stand up?"

In the last 30 years scholars have spent an enormous amount of time and energy studying Jesus of Nazareth from a purely historical perspective. There is a good chance that the real Jesus was not like most people imagine. On one end of the spectrum there is the Jesus of popular Evangelical Christianity. Some Evangelicals seem to think of Jesus as their "co-pilot" or buddy, the epitome of understanding and tolerance. They often treat him as if he were a heavenly Santa Claus who exists solely to grant their wishes. "Sweet Jesus" or "Beautiful One" are words sometimes sung in worship of him. This observation is not necessarily a criticism of the songs, but rather to point out that the real Jesus was much more down to earth.

The real Jesus was an itinerant Jewish prophet, which meant that he and his disciples traveled from town to town along dirty, dusty, and sometimes muddy roads. Bathing was a luxury that Jesus and his disciples probably rarely enjoyed, so they were often dirty, sweaty, and stinky.

It is unlikely that "sweet" or "beautiful" were among the first words that came to mind when encountering Jesus on one of those roads.[1] In other words, the image of a nicely groomed and squeaky clean Caucasian Jesus exists only in imagination.

On the other end of the spectrum, the "historical Jesus" proposed by some scholars is no less a product of imagination. Albert Schweitzer[2] recognized long ago that many Jesus scholars simply re-imagine Jesus in their own image. That hasn't changed since Schweitzer's time. Modern scholars with a cynical bent often imagine a cynical Jesus. Those with mystical leanings imagine a mystical Jesus. Scholars inclined toward social activism may imagine Jesus as a revolutionary or zealot. What many of these scholars have in common is that they approach the earliest sources seeking to find evidence to support their own perspective. Then they come up with clever ways to explain away all the evidence that undermines their view. As a result, we have numerous conflicting theories about what the historical Jesus was like. Readers may want to cry out, "Will the real Jesus please stand up?"

If the earliest historical sources[3] were allowed to speak for themselves, however, the following broad picture would emerge: Jesus was an itinerant Jewish preacher/prophet—on this virtually all scholars agree. Early Jewish prophets, like Elijah or Isaiah, for example, were known for calling people to turn from their sins back to God, and Jesus was no different in this respect. Among the sins he specifically condemned were "evil thoughts, sexual immorality, theft, murder, adultery, greed, malice, deceit, lewdness, envy, slander, arrogance and folly."[4] In Jesus' famous "Sermon on the Mount" he even addressed sinful attitudes like hypocrisy, self-righteousness, lust, hatred and refusal to forgive others.[5]

Jesus was generally known for his kindness and compassion but he was also a fiery preacher of judgment. He called religious leaders of his day "whitewashed tombs," "snakes," "hypocrites" and "sons of hell!"[6] In fact he condemned his entire generation, saying that hell would be worse for them than for Sodom and Gomorrah since "from everyone who has been given much, much will be demanded."[7] Two of our earliest sources, therefore, began their story of Jesus' public ministry with Jesus calling his generation to repentance.[8]

Many fiery preachers, however, have been lost to history. Among the things that made Jesus so memorable were the shocking claims that led to his death. In fact, because of these claims, Jesus was accused by Jewish authorities of blasphemy and was turned over to the Romans on charges of sedition![9]

According to our earliest sources, the blasphemy charges came from the fact that Jesus' words and actions implied that he thought of himself as nothing less than the embodiment of God! For example in one source, Jesus is said to have claimed God as his Father, saying "I and my Father are one," and "Anyone who has seen me has seen the Father."[10] That Jesus actually held this view is collaborated by other sources in which he is said to have claimed things for himself that in his culture were only believed to be true of God. For example, he claimed to be able to grant forgiveness of sin,[11] and that he was "lord" of the Sabbath Day.[12] He claimed that he would one day judge the living and the dead at the final judgment.[13] The Jews in Jesus' culture believed these things were only true of God. That Jesus' opponents understood exactly what he was claiming is clear from the fact that on more than one occasion they unsuccessfully attempted to kill him for blasphemy because, in their words, "you, a mere man, claim to be God."[14] Blasphemy was one of the charges against Jesus at his trial.

Of course the Romans who ruled the country would care nothing about Jewish religious concerns of blasphemy so the religious leaders needed something that would get the attention of the Roman governor. Instead of charging Jesus with blasphemy, therefore, they sent him to the governor on charges of sedition. Jewish people in Jesus' time were expecting a military or political messiah or Christ; a "king of kings" to deliver them from their oppressive Roman occupiers. Since the Romans would probably have imprisoned or executed anyone publicly claiming to be a messiah, Jesus was careful about how he approached this topic in public—but the messiah is precisely who he claimed to be during his trials.[15] The Jewish leadership, therefore, sent him to the Roman governor on charges of sedition, i.e. for claiming to be "King of the Jews." The Roman governor ordered that Jesus be tortured to death by nailing him alive to a cross.

We might have expected that this would be the end of the story. After all, there was nothing out of the ordinary about the crucifixion of Jewish "troublemakers"—literally thousands of Jews were crucified in the first century. More importantly, others had also claimed to be messiahs, but when they were executed their movements always died with them. That is because many Jewish people thought the messiah would deliver Israel from foreign rule. It was simply assumed that an executed "messiah" could not possibly have been genuine. So we might have expected the story to end with Jesus' crucifixion.

In Jesus' case, however, not only did his followers continue to believe even after his death, but the Jesus movement actually grew significantly! In fact, these followers even began worshipping Jesus—something truly surprising in a monotheistic culture that believed in only one God!

All of this raises the question of why anyone would continue to believe in, much less worship, an apparently failed messiah who had been crucified. Crucifixion, after all, was considered a very shameful way to die, so getting someone to believe in a crucified messiah would be a huge obstacle, not to mention a terrible marketing strategy!

It is not surprising, therefore, that most people did *not* believe in Jesus. His enemies thought he was a blasphemer or demon possessed or even crazy— which is exactly what one might expect of someone who made the kind of claims about himself that Jesus reportedly made. In other words, the story makes sense from a historical perspective.

Those who continued to believe in Jesus after his death did so for several reasons. First, they were convinced that Jesus had performed extraordinary miracles. There are no ancient records of anyone denying that Jesus had done such amazing things. His enemies claimed that his miracles were sorcery or magic. His followers were well aware of traveling magicians but countered that no one had ever done the kinds of amazing signs and wonders Jesus had done.

Second, Jesus' earliest followers believed in him because they were convinced that he had fulfilled Jewish prophecies. For example, they believed that Jesus' birth in Bethlehem, his lineage from King David, his miracles, and numerous events surrounding his death and burial were all fulfillments of ancient prophecies of a coming messiah.

Finally, Jesus' followers believed in him because they were absolutely convinced that he had come back to life after having been dead and entombed. The earliest sources do not portray this as merely a vision or a hallucination. They say Jesus' disciples conversed with him, ate with him and even touched him after his resurrection. Even highly skeptical scholars generally agree that the earliest followers of Jesus were absolutely convinced that he had risen from the dead. The skeptics are quick to add, however, that this is impossible since dead people never come back to life. Other scholars charge that the skeptics' conclusions are based on their worldview, not on history or evidence.

Christians later in the first century could also point to the fact that Jesus had accurately predicted the destruction of Jerusalem and its temple, which came to pass forty years after his death. So for whatever reasons, Jesus' followers were so convinced that he really was who he claimed to be that they risked everything, including imprisonment, torture, and even death to follow him.

But what did it mean to *follow* a messiah who was no longer physically with them? Did following Jesus mean growing a beard, eating kosher food and living off the donations of the wealthy women who had followed and supported him? Hardly! Following Jesus meant obeying his commands. Jesus taught, "If you love me you will obey what I command."[16] Indeed, the last recorded command Jesus gave to his followers was to make disciples, "teaching them to obey all things I have commanded you."[17]

So what were some of those commands? Jesus taught that people must repent of their sinfulness. They must love God even more than they love to live and they must love their neighbors— and even their enemies—as they love themselves. Jesus expected his followers to treat others as they themselves would want to be treated. His followers were to strive to live a lifestyle of compassion, love, generosity, forgiveness, worship and prayer. They were to be honest, ethical, moral and merciful. They were to encourage others, make peace and make disciples. They were to avoid sin at all costs and to sincerely repent when they failed!

But following Jesus went deeper than just obeying some rules. Jesus taught his disciples that love for God and his kingdom was to be their highest priority. Jesus taught that God's kingdom was even more important than their closest relatives and loved ones. On this much even most skeptical scholars agree. What some miss, however, is that Jesus claimed to be the king of that kingdom. Putting the kingdom first, meant putting the King first—and Jesus and his followers believed that Jesus was that King.

With teaching like this, it is no wonder that Jesus's enemies thought he was crazy, and it is no wonder that the Romans crucified him for sedition. It is also no wonder that those who believed in him would lay down their lives for him and await his promised return. Again, the story makes perfect sense from a historical perspective.

But there is more. Jesus taught that unless people's righteousness exceeded that of the scribes and Pharisees, they

would not enter the kingdom of God.
That was difficult for most of Jesus'
contemporaries to comprehend because
Pharisees were respected religious leaders
who strived to keep all the rules—and
some were apparently quite proud of it
as they self-righteously looked down their
noses at others!

For example, Jesus once told a story
about a Pharisee and a tax collector who
went to the temple to pray. In those days
people looked up to Pharisees but they
hated tax collectors who were hired to
collect taxes for the Roman occupiers. In
Jesus' story the Pharisee bragged about
fasting twice a week and giving money to
the poor. The Pharisee thanked God that
he was not like that sinful tax collector.
The tax collector, on the other hand,
beat his chest in remorse crying "God
be merciful to me a sinner." Surprisingly,
Jesus said it was not the Pharisee but the
tax collector who was declared right with
God![18] The moral of this story is that those

who self-righteously come to God thinking they are good enough for God are not good enough and will not enter God's kingdom. Jesus taught that those who are "justified" or declared to be in right standing with God are those who come to God humbly confessing their sin and who follow Jesus in faith.

People often misunderstand the nature of this faith. The faith of which Jesus spoke was more than just mental agreement with some doctrines or dogmas. Faith involves the attitude of the heart. One of the early sources about Jesus contains a story of how Jesus was sharing a meal with a group of religious leaders when suddenly a woman came in. The woman was crying. Since she was described as a sinner in the story (four times!),[19] since no other reason for the tears were given, and since the ultimate result was forgiveness of her sins, readers are led to believe that the woman was sorrowfully repentant for her sin. The woman ignored the religious leaders and went straight to Jesus. Showing remarkable humility and devotion, she got down on her knees as she kissed Jesus's feet, anointed them with ointment and wiped them with her hair.

The host, a Pharisee named Simon, was indignant: If Jesus were a prophet, surely he would know this woman was a sinner, and he wouldn't allow her to touch him! Jesus pointed out that when he had come in to Simon's house, Simon had not even extended the basic courtesies of hospitality to Jesus, whereas this woman had washed Jesus' feet with her tears, wiped them with her hair and anointed them with oil. Jesus said, "Therefore I tell you, her sins, which are many, are forgiven—for she loved much." Then he told the woman that *her faith* had saved her.[20]

But wait! What faith? Nothing in this story said anything about faith.

The story leads readers to understand that this woman's sorrowful repentance over her sin, coupled with her loving devotion to Jesus, is the very definition of the kind of faith necessary to enter the kingdom about which Jesus had so often preached. The actions of the woman were outward expressions of a heart of faith. The concept of faith, therefore, is very simple. It is about a relationship in which we—like the woman in the story—respond to Jesus in genuine repentance for our sin and with a heart of loving devotion to Jesus.

Like salt, faith is very simple, but just as a simple substance like salt can be broken down into the elements from which it is composed, so also saving faith can be analyzed and broken down into parts. First, saving faith includes repentance. Repentance is a "no excuses" attitude that involves coming to grips with the fact that our sin is not just a mistake, or the result of our environment, or someone else's fault. Repentance involves a humble and sorrowful acknowledgement that we have willfully sinned against a holy God, combined with a desire to live a life that pleases him.

Second, saving faith involves recognition that our sin has destroyed our relationship with God and no amount of good works on our part will ever make it right. If we are going to be saved from the wrath of God at the final judgment, about which Jesus warned, it will only be by God's mercy and grace. Like the story of the Pharisee in the temple, as long as we think we are good enough for God, we will not enter God's kingdom.

Third, Jesus believed that his death would bring about forgiveness of sins for his followers.[21] Jesus and his followers seemed to believe that he was fulfilling an ancient Jewish prophecy about a "servant" of God who would be "pierced for our transgressions" or sin, and whose death would "justify many."[22] Faith involves recognition that Jesus' death on that cross was not just Roman cruelty but was the "ransom"[23] to pay the penalty for our sin so we could be "justified" or declared right with God.

Finally, faith involves a heart response of loving devotion to Jesus as the only one who can fix our broken relationship with God. This "love" is not some kind of gushy sentimentalism that imagines us snuggling up in Jesus' lap or some such nonsense. It is more like the undying devotion a soldier might have toward a respected general or leader. In the book, *Lone Survivor*, the author, a navy SEAL, describes one of his instructors, saying, "We loved him, all of us, because we all sensed he truly wanted the best for us."[24] The reader is left with the impression that the kind of loving devotion these men had for their instructor would have led them to go anywhere, endure anything, and even lay down their lives for him! This is the kind of loving devotion we are to have toward Jesus who laid down his life for us![25] This kind of faith involves swearing allegiance, so to speak, to Jesus as the King and highest authority in our life.

This faith can be expressed in a simple prayer: "Lord Jesus, I have sinned against you in thoughts, words, actions and even attitudes. I don't want to live a lifestyle that grieves you anymore. Please forgive me of my sin. Come into my life, be my King, change me and make me the kind of person you want me to be."

Just mouthing the words to a prayer doesn't save anyone, of course, but if this prayer sincerely expresses the attitude of your heart, the Bible says your sins have been forgiven, you have been "justified" or declared right with God and you are now part of the kingdom of God. As the apostle Paul once wrote, "Therefore there is now no condemnation for those who are in Christ Jesus."[26]

So what's next?

First, find a church where the Bible is preached (hint: if you don't need to refer to the Bible regularly during the sermon, you may want to look for another church). You need to be associated with other believers to grow in your faith. Let the pastor know you are a new Christian and want to grow.

Second, ask your new pastor to baptize you. We don't get baptized in order to be saved—the only thing required for salvation is faith, but the idea of an unbaptized Christian would have been unthinkable to the earliest Christians. Baptism is the initial outward expression of your faith and a public indication that you are serious about your commitment to Christ.

Third, start developing a life of prayer. Prayer is not nearly as complicated as many people make it out to be. Prayer is just talking to God like you would talk to a friend. You don't need to use special religious language. You don't even need to talk out loud. Just talk. You can talk to God anytime, anyplace, about anything.

Fourth, start reading the earliest sources about Jesus for yourself. You'll find most of them conveniently collected in the New Testament of the Bible. If you get a good "study Bible," the notes will help you better understand what you are reading. Your new pastor can recommend a good study Bible.

Finally, as you read your Bible strive to put into practice what you learn about living in obedience to Jesus the King.[27] We don't strive to please God in order to be saved. We strive to please God in gratitude and loving response to his mercy and love.

Endnotes

1   Cf. Isaiah 53:2.

2   1875-1965.

3   Nearly all scholars agree that the earliest sources about Jesus—all written in the first century AD when Jesus lived—are 1) the letters of the apostle Paul, 2) the Four Gospels collected in the New Testament, 3) a lost Gospel we now call Q, though some scholars doubt this ever existed, 4) other letters collected in the New Testament, 5) two short passages written by a Jewish historian named Josephus and 5) a letter written by Clement of Rome. Nearly all scholars agree that virtually all of the so-called "lost gospels" come from at least 100 to 300 (or more) years after Jesus' time and are of little to no value in reconstructing the life of the historical Jesus.

4   Mark 7:21-22.

5   Matthew 5:1-7:28.

6   Matthew 23.

7   Matthew 10: 15; Luke 12:48.

8   Mark 1:15; Matthew 4:17.

9   Mark 14:64; Luke 23:2-3.

10   John 10:10; John 14:9.

11   Mark 2:1-12.

12   Mark 2:23-28.

13   Matthew 25:31-46.

14   John 10:33

15   Mark 14:61-62; Luke 23:3.

16   John 14:15, 21, 23, 24; 15:10, 14.

17   Matthew 28:19-20.

18   Luke 18:9-14.

19   Luke 7:37; 39; 47, 48.

20   Luke 7:36-50.

21   Mark 10:45; Matthew 26:26-29

22   Isaiah 53

23   Mark 10:45

24   Marcus Luttrell. *Lone Survivor*. New York: Back Bay Books, 2007, 109.

25   Mark 8:34-37; Matthew 10:37-29, Luke 14:26-27, John 12:25-26.

26   Romans 8:1.

27   Colossians 1:10; 1 Thessalonians 4:1; Hebrews 3:20-21.

About the Author

Dennis Ingolfsland is the Director of Library Services and a full-professor of Bible at Crown College in Minnesota. Ordained with the North American Baptist Conference, he has a B.A. in biblical languages from Calvary Bible College, an M.A. in Library Science from the University of Missouri, an M.A. in theological Studies from Fuller Theological Seminary and a D.Phil. in Religion and Society from Oxford Graduate School in Tennessee.

Dr. Ingolfsland is the author of *The Least of the Apostles* and *I Pledge Allegiance to the King* as well as numerous articles and book reviews.

CPSIA information can be obtained
at www.ICGtesting.com
Printed in the USA
LVOW10s0924080617
537369LV00013B/405/P